Cuban Kids

George Ancona

MARSHALL CAVENDISH • NEW YORK

Library of Congress Card Number: 00-102258
ISBN 0-7614-5077-7

The text of this book is set in 14 point Berkeley Old Style Medium.
Printed in Hong Kong
First edition

6 5 4 3 2 1

To Susan Pearson

Author's Note

As a boy I dreamed of going to far-off places. In sixth grade we studied Cuba and I built a little sugar cane cart. When I grew up I figured that if I became a photographer I could travel and see the places I had read about.

In 1957 I went to Cuba with my camera. I roamed the streets and alleys of old Havana. Because of the camera I was able to stop and talk to strangers, take their pictures and get to know them.

The revolution was already underway. Fidel Castro, Che Guevara and their small band of rebels were fighting in the mountains. Havana was an armed camp. Soldiers armed with machine guns were on every corner. After a week I left and returned home.

On New Year's Day 1959, Che Guevara, Camilo Cienfuegos and their ragged army marched into Havana and were welcomed by thousands of cheering *Habaneros*. Fidel Castro proclaimed that the revolution would take the path of socialism. The new government announced that education and medicine would be free for everyone. They also took over foreign industries. In response, the United States imposed an embargo, cutting off the island from any American exports, visitors and business. Forty years have gone by. Castro is still in power and the embargo is still in place.

During those years I began to write children's books. I was curious to see how Cuba had changed so I proposed to my editor that we do a book on Cuba. I wanted to show how children grow up in Cuba.

Well, here it is.

George Ancona

*T*he rat-tat-tat of military drums fills the quiet streets of Majagua, a town in central Cuba. Schoolchildren, teachers, and towns-people are parading to celebrate the birthday of José Martí. In Cuba this day is celebrated the way we celebrate the Fourth of July.

A little boy wearing a straw hat, a cardboard machete, and a *guayabera*, the traditional Cuban shirt, leads the parade and carries the Cuban flag. He is dressed as a *guajiro*, one of the Cuban peasants who fought in the revolutionary wars.

One little girl carries a picture of José Martí, a writer and poet who called for a *Cuba Libre*, a free Cuba, independent from Spain. For this he was exiled from Cuba in 1880. He was seventeen years old.

For the next fifteen years he lived and wrote in Mexico, Spain, and the United States. In 1895 he returned to Cuba with an army of exiled Cubans to begin the revolution. He was killed in his first battle. The event is commemorated with a statue in Central Park in New York. His poetry lives on today in the lyrics of the popular Cuban song, *Guantanamera*.

Schoolchildren are called *pioneros* and wear uniforms. Grades one to three wear red neckerchiefs—grades four to six wear blue. Secondary school students, grades seven to nine, wear yellow pants and skirts. The procession gathers at the statue of José Martí where the students place flowers.

Martí was particularly interested in the well-being and education of children. He wrote, *Nada hay mas importante que un niño*—There is nothing more important than a child.

After the parade, children perform traditional folk dances. Boys dressed as guajiros dance with girls dressed in red, white and blue, the colors of the Cuban flag. One girl wears a kite and dances to the tugging of an imaginary string held by her partner.

A short drive from Majagua is a small farming community of three hundred people. Cuba is dotted with many similar communities. The people who live here are the *campesinos*, the country people who raise the foods that keep Cuba alive.

Here, there is only a one-room schoolhouse for children from the first to the third grade. After that they go by bus to a larger school in Majagua. *Maestro* Luís, the teacher, was born in this village. He left to study at the university, then returned to teach the children of his home town.

His lessons include the history of the 1959 Revolution and how it changed their country. In 1956 a small band of exiled Cubans led by Fidel Castro returned to Cuba from Mexico on a small yacht called the *Granma*.

Many were killed when they landed but the survivors fled to the mountains. The rebels swelled to an army of 50,000 *compañeros*, the men and women who were comrades in arms. Today Cubans greet each other with the title of compañero or compañera.

After the day's lessons, Maestro Luís hangs a *piñata* to celebrate the six children with birthdays this month. Each holds a string attached to the piñata. When Maestro Luís shouts *Jale!*, the children pull and the *caramelos* spill to the floor.

Some of the mothers made a huge cake with candles which the children blow out. Then the class settles down to eat.

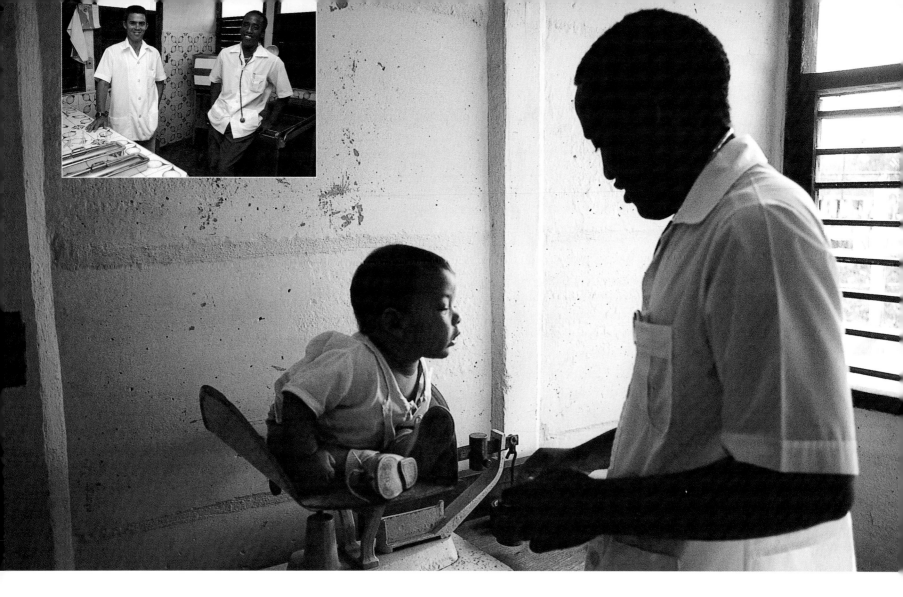

Just a little way down the street stands a small cinder block building where the town's doctor and nurse live and work. Anyone who is sick can go to see them at any time of the day or night. In Cuba all medical services are free. Cuban doctors' biggest problem is the shortage of medicines.

Because of the fall of communism in Europe in 1989, Cuba lost the support of those countries. This, together with the American embargo, created many shortages in Cuba. Food, gasoline, and other goods are rationed.

The sugar cane that grows in fields surrounding the village is exported to many countries in exchange for manufactured goods.

Before a field of sugar cane is harvested, campesinos come to cut and collect the leaves to feed their animals. After school a boy helps his father load the leaves into their cart.

In the morning a combine begins to harvest the sugar cane. It gathers the entire plant, cuts it into pieces, blows the leaves out the back and loads the cane onto a truck. Clouds of white egrets follow the combine to feed on the uncovered worms and insects. If a field is too uneven or has been burned, campesinos cut the cane by hand with *machetes*.

For lunch the harvesting crew heads for the chuck wagon where a cook prepares a hearty meal of rice, pumpkin, beans, yucca, and bread. The old people of Cuba remember the hunger, sickness and illiteracy of the campesinos that existed before the revolution. Today the state runs all the farms and campesinos have year-round work and pay.

Short of fuel, fertilizers, insecticides, and spare parts, farmers are replacing tractors with oxen and returning to organic farming. In both city gardens and country farms, Cubans are growing chemical-free produce which people can buy directly from the growers.

José Martí believed that a child's education should include the love of work. After school, students work on organic farms for extra credit.

Because of the paper shortage Alfredo Zaldívar uses recycled materials to publish hand-made books in the city of Matanzas. He also publishes a magazine of children's writings. The words and pictures are printed on scrap paper with old mimeograph machines. Then the pages are torn or cut and sewn together.

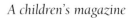

A children's magazine

The covers are made of scrap cardboard. Only two hundred books of each title are published. On a school holiday a mother brings her son to watch how she assembles an edition. These books have become known around the world as works of art.

Mella is a town that grew around a sugar refinery. Alongside the refinery stands the town's elementary school. Every morning the students gather in the school's courtyard in order to pledge allegiance to the flag. They end with a shout of *Seremos como Che!*—We will be like Che!

Che Guevara was the young Argentine doctor who joined Fidel Castro to fight in the Cuban Revolution. He had traveled throughout Latin America and had seen the misery of the poor and decided to try to make changes.

Mornings are devoted to academic studies. Outside, freight cars filled with sugar begin their long journey to other countries. Yisel's teacher helps her with a geometry problem. When the morning classes are over, the students run home for lunch.

Yisel lives with her family, which includes her brother, sister, mother, father, grandmother, grandfather, and great grandmother. Her favorite sport is baseball. She plays her own version by kicking a baggy old basketball. Later, in the shade of her porch, Yisel plays pattycake with her friend. At night she likes to read books.

One of Yisel's classmates is Blas. As soon as he gets home, off comes the uniform, shoes, and socks. First he runs to the store to buy some groceries for his mother, who is expecting a baby. Like most men of the town, Blas's father works at the mill. After his errand Blas heads out to play baseball with his friends. The equipment is makeshift but that doesn't keep them from having fun.

Georgina lives with her mother, sister, grandfather, and grandmother. She loves to listen to her grandfather talk about his life.

"Before the Revolution", explains *Abuelo*, "here, all there was for children was a playground. The best houses were for the American bosses. Then there were the houses for the office workers or mechanics and then came the humble houses for the laborers.

People lived in separate neighborhoods and did not speak to each other. Blacks were separated from whites and there was much racism. We rented the house from the company but after the Revolution the houses were given to the workers. Now this is my house and when I die my family can stay here."

"Back then kids went to school only until the sixth grade because they had to work. Even though my mother wanted me to study I had to work. I have two younger sisters though, who, after the Revolution, became doctors."

"Now there is a secondary school and a pre-university school in town. Those who complete the *pre* go on to study at a university. I have two daughters who are also doctors and one who is a biologist—Georgina's mother. My sons are all technicians. And it hasn't cost me a penny."

Every city has a *Palacio de los Pioneros*, or Palace of the Pioneers, a building where children are taken after school. In Santiago, the second biggest city in Cuba, the government turned the mansion of a rich man who left the country into a palacio. Here children can take any classes that interest them. There are classes in agriculture, art, cooking, construction, sports, music, medicine, science, fishing, and many other professions.

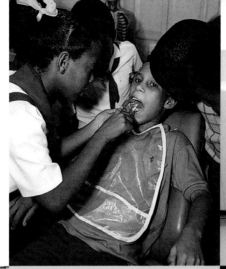

Dentistry
Computers
Auto Mechanics
Military
Teaching
Sewing

On their way home from school, Dairon and Lialne's grandfather, Edilberto, meets them and they walk home together. Abuelo Edilberto is a musician who teaches young people to play traditional Cuban music. Dairon and Lialne quickly change from their school uniforms and join the group in the front parlor. Dairon plays the *bongos* and cow bell and Lialne sings and plays the *claves*.

"A few years ago I got very sick," explains Abuelo, "I was in the hospital a long time. The doctors took very good care of me and I got better.

When I got home I began to think about how I could pass on my music to my grandchildren. I decided to form a group of neighborhood kids. They all study music in school and can play anything, but I knew the traditional rhythms. This is what I can pass on."

"Before, a child who was interested in music needed a parent or godfather to pay for the lessons. Today we have centers where kids can go to study music, use the instruments and perform—all for free."

Cubans love baseball. All over the country barefooted kids play baseball on any open street or in any park. *Habana* has a big stadium where teams from all over the country come to play. This is where an American team recently played a Cuban team for the first time in many years.

Havana is the capital of Cuba and its largest city. Old Havana is the beautiful colonial section. There are many museums where students are taken. Not many people have automobiles and many cars date back to the early 1950's, before the Revolution. Gasoline is very expensive and limited. So most people ride bikes, motorcycles, tricycles, hitchhike, or squeeze into double-bodied buses called *camellos*. Cubans say, "We may have little, but it's ours."

In Cuba children are very protected. After school, on weekends, and holidays, children can go to Havana's Palace of the Pioneers, named after Che Guevara. The Palace is located in Lenin Park, a huge park at the edge of the city.

Children put on shows in the central courtyard. Around the courtyard are classrooms, shops, and laboratories where children explore their interests. The three pools are an inviting treat on hot summer days.

An old Russian railroad engine with open cars takes children for a ride around the park. There is also an amusement area where children can ride horses, bikes, and a variety of rides.

Elementary schoolchildren can take dance as one of their school subjects. Boys and girls study classical ballet, modern dance, or Spanish Flamenco.

Another of the specialized high schools is the school for the circus. In Cuba the circus is considered an art form. Students who graduate are assured a job with one of the traveling circuses.

A children's folk dance group rehearses in the courtyard of a *solár*, a maze of apartments built into an existing old building. Each child represents one of the *orishas*, or gods in the Yoruba religion from Africa.

Yemayá is the goddess of the sea and queen of the world. *Ochún* is the goddess of the river and sweet waters. When they dance they imitate the movements of water by waving their skirts.

Chango is the god of lightning and thunder, his symbol is the ax. *Obatalá* is the goddess of peace, love, and health. *Elegguá* is the orisha who clears the way and gives candy to children.

Oyá is the goddess of the wind and cemeteries. *Yabo*, who dresses in white, will one day become a priestess. *Oggún* is the lord of iron, metals and tools.

Oggún

   Drummers play while neighbors gather to sing and clap among the clotheslines. As dusk approaches, the drums and singing attract neighbors to their windows and balconies to look down upon the dancing children in the courtyard.

   Despite the hardships, the shortages, and the embargo, Cuban kids are growing up with a love of their country, traditions, and culture. Their many skills will contribute to making a better future for Cuba and the world.

Glossary

abuelo grandfather

bongo two small drums held between the knees

camello a camel, a Cuban double bus

campesino a rural person

caramelo candy

Che Argentine slang expression, *Hey! Man!*

claves two hardwood sticks used as a musical instrument

compañero companion, friend, comrade in arms

Cuba Libre a free Cuba

embargo a prohibition of trade

flamenco a traditional Spanish music and dance

gracias thank you

Granma name of yacht used in revolution

guajiro a Cuban peasant

guayabera a loose fitting men's shirt

Habana Havana

Habaneros residents of Havana

jale pull

machete a large heavy knife

maestro teacher

orishas deities

palacio palace

piñata decorated container of sweets that is broken by children

pioneros pioneers, Cuban students

pre preparatory school

Santiago de Cuba easternmost city in Cuba

solár Cuban tenement

Acknowledgments

Gracias to the many people who helped me find my way through a network of friends both in and out of Cuba:

Stuart Ashman, Director of the Museum of Fine Arts in Santa Fe, NM, Judith Bettelheim, The Center for Cuban Studies in NY, Jorge Rivas Rodríguez of Trabajadores, Carlos Vega, Nancy Figueras Silvera of Museo de Educación, Nina Menendez, Pablo Menendez, Adriana Santana, Fela Maizosa, Eduardo Veitia of the Ballet Espanol de Habana, Silvia Rodriguez of the Escuela Elemental de Ballet, Santica Maldonado Alfonso of the Grupo Aché Iya Lucum, Rosa María López and Raúl Niebo Santiesteba of the Instituto Cubano de Amistad con los Pueblos, Alexis Guedes Denis of Majagua, Luís Gomez of Victoria de Girón, Berto Ruano and Onelio Silveira Vaillant of the Centro Cultural El Batey, Alfredo Zaldivar of Ediciones Vigía. And Marina Ancona for her assistance and the photograph on page 7.